"37 Quick Tips to Help You Thrive as a New Mom"

"Feel Confident, Care for Your Baby, and Get the Sleep You Deserve!"

Special <u>FREE</u> Bonus Gift forYou

To help you to achieve more sleep success, there
are **FREE BONUS RESOURCES** for you at:

www.FreeGiftFromNesta.com

- Claim your free Baby Sleep Strategy Session
  (VALUE $500) with my team

Nesta Lumpkin ®

What others are saying about Nesta

"If you're ready to positively transform your life, then read and absorb the strategies in this brilliant book by Nesta Lumpkin! Nesta has written a guide to help you go from where you are to where you want to be and her strategies will have you living a life full of purpose and passion!"

–James Malinchak

Featured on ABC's Hit TV Show, *"Secret Millionaire"* (Viewed by 50 Million+ Worldwide)

Authored 27 Books, Delivered 3,000 Presentations & 2,000 Consultations Best-Selling Author, *Millionaire Success Secrets*

Founder, www.BigMoneySpeaker.com

"After joining the Baby Sleep Accelerator™ Coaching Program, people at work are like, "Oh my gosh… it's working like I mean, you're, like, happier now here!". And I was like, I know because I'm actually sleeping. I could actually feel like a human again. My wife and I have a plan, and we know exactly what to do when our baby wakes up during the night. We have a game plan. We have the blueprint that Nesta shared with us."

–Nathan Cooper. Baby Sleep Accelerator™ Coaching Insider.

"So our fourth baby was sleeping great until four months, and then she stopped sleeping great and was waking up every couple hours. Honestly, the Baby Sleep Accelerator™ Coaching Program worked so fast for us. Like, I mean, it was the first week.

–Kellie Berry. Baby Sleep Accelerator™ Coaching Insider.

"From a business standpoint the return on investment relative to the baby going to sleep is huge. And so, you might be hesitant in the beginning just as Kelly said and things like that. But once you start to see the results and you stay consistent with the program …It works!"

–Matthew Berry. Baby Sleep Accelerator™ Coaching Insider.

"I feel that I have gained a lot more of the confidence through the Baby Sleep Accelerator™ Coaching Program as we were able to apply different methods, but also methods that were, just kind of unique to what my baby's needs were, and what, you know, we felt comfortable doing. And with consistency, he's now sleeping a lot better ...which is incredible!"

–Priscilla Perez. Baby Sleep Accelerator™ Coaching Insider.

"Nesta's strategies could be the key to your baby's sleep success. It was for me." My husband and I had not slept in the same bed since my daughter was born because one of us had to sleep in her room with her. Nesta's sessions were encouraging. The food section was the most helpful part of the downloadable checklist."

–Sonnia Ragozin. Baby Sleep Accelerator™ Coaching Insider.

"Nesta comes at this topic as both a committed, hard-working mom and a journalist who wants to empower everyone to face this challenge head on! "

— Josh Levs. Keynoter. Top Expert in All In Workplaces & Modern Dads.

"Nesta is the bomb diggity because of what she's talking about for getting my baby to sleep through the night!

— Nicole Celso. Baby Sleep Accelerator™ Coaching Insider.

"I was able to use Nesta as a baby coach or a mommy coach to help me with my daughter, Eden, when we were trying to get her own sleep training. Eden has been sleep training and sleeping through the night for about twelve to thirteen hours since February of this year. She is now fourteen months. And Nesta was a huge help when it came to sleep training our daughter.

— Tia Miller. Baby Sleep Accelerator™ Coaching Insider.

"Nesta I can't thank you enough for your program. The entire process was amazing but your one-on-one coaching was key for us. After two days our baby boy is able to sleep through the night."

— Tolu Ekhaesomhi. Baby Sleep Accelerator™ Coaching Insider.

"Nesta Lumpkin has an exceptional talent for identifying and addressing the unique sleep challenges faced by infants. Her personalized approach goes beyond mere techniques, as she imbues a sense of confidence and calm in parents, which is crucial in navigating the often-challenging early stages of parenthood. The impact of her work is profound. She restores joy and brings much-needed time freedom to overworked and frustrated moms and dads. In a world where parental burnout is all too common, Nesta's work is not just a service but a lifeline to many families."

–Muhsinah Morris, Ph.D. CEO and Founder, Metaverse United. Director. Senior Assistant Professor at Morehouse College.

"Nesta is such a highly driven, inspirational, mother who's making an impact through proven methods. Her methods not only help your baby sleep, but provide a better-quality life for families, a healthier child, and a promising future full of productivity. Sleep is one of the most essential elements for a healthy body, mind and overall wellbeing. Nesta has provided exemplary tools that I myself have used to help my two children sleep, which helped provide a functional lifestyle that was enjoyable for all. This book is your recipe for success and sets you up for a easier transition into motherhood."

–Dr. Tawanna Ojo, MBA, MS.

"Nesta goes above and beyond for her own children. She teaches them the power of having a growth mindset. She is an advocate for babies to get the benefits from sleep."

–Esther Alonge Family Care Expert.

MOTIVATE AND INSPIRE OTHERS!

"Share This Book"

Retail $15.95

Special Quantity

5-20 Books	$12.95
21-99 Books	$10.95
100-499 Books	$8.95
500-999 Books	$6.95
1,000+ Books	$4.95

To Place an Order Contact:

info@nestalumpkin.com

404-836-3830

THE IDEAL PROFESSIONAL SPEAKER FOR YOUR NEXT EVENT!

Any organization that wants to develop their people to become "extraordinary," needs to hire Nesta Lumpkin for a keynote and/or workshop training!

TO CONTACT OR BOOK NESTA LUMPKIN
admin@nestaspeaks.com

TO SPEAK:

404-836-3830

THE IDEAL COACH AND CONSULTANT FOR YOU!

If you're ready to overcome challenges, have major breakthroughs and achieve higher levels, then you will love having Nesta Lumpkin as your coach!

TO CONTACT OR BOOK NESTA LUMPKIN
info@babysleepaccelerator.com
404-836-3830
www.nestalumpkin.com

Dedication

It is with respect, admiration, and sincere appreciation, that I dedicate this book to my wonderful family: Team Lumpkin. Without you and the lessons you have taught me throughout my life, I would not have the blessing of being where I am today. Thank you from the bottom of my heart!I love you dearly!

TABLE OF CONTENTS

INCREASE YOUR EFFICIENCY

BABY CARE

A Message to You!

You're likely reading this because you're expecting a baby, have recently welcomed one, or have become a parent through adoption or surrogacy. Either way, welcome to the world of parenting! These tips are intended to complement the standard items typically found on a baby essentials list and the usual advice you receive when preparing for a new arrival.

While no one has all the answers to make parenting a completely smooth journey, this book will help make your first year with your new baby much easier. It's packed with practical things you can do now to make the first months and years as a new parent more manageable.

The first months after having a baby can be tough on your mind, body, and soul. This period, known as postpartum, is often challenging. The Centers for Disease Control defines it as the first six to eight weeks after birth, but it can last much longer. This is partly due to the sharp drop in certain hormones that affect your mood. When these hormones are out of balance, it can lead to anything from extreme anxiety about your baby to a lack of interest in caring for them.

The postpartum period is like navigating a minefield. It's a critical time when the health and well-being of both mom and baby are essential for them to thrive.

You may have heard stories about what postpartum is like, but the truth is, no one can predict the hidden challenges you'lll face during this time.

Postpartum is like high school graduation. It's the subject of many books, TV shows, and movies, but no one can fully explain what it will feel like for you until you actually walk across that stage and receive your diploma. No one else's words can truly capture what it's like to take it home and realize that this chapter of your life is over, and a new one is beginning.

For some women, the postpartum period goes smoothly. But for many, it can feel like driving blindfolded down a dirt road filled with potholes, without a map. Suddenly, postpartum depression appears in the backseat. A few miles later, postpartum anxiety is hitchhiking on the side of the road.

Now, imagine this car is full of buttons and gadgets you've never seen before, and you're expected to figure them all out instantly so you can hit the road. It's like getting into a new car and being expected to master all the controls immediately. That's how it can feel to juggle breastfeeding, formula feeding, newborn sleep, bathing, diaper changes, self-care, household management, and maybe even a career. Through all of this, you must keep your eyes on the road to avoid crashing under the pressure.

After you have a baby, something interesting happens. It's like you become a less important version of yourself, almost invisible. It seems like people expect you to put everyone else first and put yourself last. But that's not how it should be. You should always be kind to yourself and love yourself. You have the right to take care of yourself, as a person, a woman, and a mom. You owe it to yourself to invest in yourself to learn more and grow every chance you get.

In 2023, Peanut released a report titled "The State of Invisibility," which explores how moms feel invisible when they become the main caregiver for their baby. Of the 3,600 moms surveyed, 95% said they felt unappreciated, unacknowledged, or unseen.

The biggest impact a new baby can have on you is the level of sleep deprivation you'll likely experience. Sleep deprivation means not getting enough sleep, and the quality of your rest takes a serious hit.

As America's #1 Baby Sleep Accelerator™ Coach, I've heard from hundreds of moms who say that their baby not sleeping through the night is the main reason they feel exhausted and overwhelmed as parents.

In 2023, Snuz, a UK baby crib maker, surveyed 1,300 parents and found that moms and dads lose 133 nights of sleep during the first year after having a baby. Losing that much sleep can seriously affect your health, leading to depression, heart problems, high blood pressure, forgetfulness, and even accidents.

These facts aren't here to scare you but to remind you to prepare as much as possible for your new baby and to prioritize self-care. Many moms don't talk about the tough times they faced after childbirth, either because they've blocked it out or don't want to overwhelm you.

If you have the resources to invest in yourself and get expert guidance through those first crucial months with a new baby, take the opportunity.

By the time your baby is four months old, you can have them sleeping through the night! Sounds easy, right? With the Baby Sleep Accelerator™ Coaching Program, it can be.

For newborns, you'll learn how to establish healthy sleep habits from day one and build up to those all-important nights of uninterrupted sleep. As a parent with an infant, helping your baby sleep through the night is the single most beneficial skill for boosting your family's health and well-being.

Showing your baby to sleep through the night helps you regain control of your time, maintain strong relationships with your spouse or partner, and makes the transition back to work much smoother.

The Baby Sleep Accelerator™ blueprint is designed to get your baby sleeping through the night quickly! I developed this approach after returning to work with each of my three children. Each of them learned to sleep up to 12 hours a night by four months old. These methods were documented and refined into a formula that many families have successfully followed.

Enjoy this book and its impactful tips. May you have more restful nights and brighter days!

Disclaimer

It is imperative that you consult with your pediatrician before initiating any form of sleep education for your infant. This book provides tips and general guidance and is not a substitute for professional medical advice. Adhering to the recommendations herein does not guarantee specific outcomes, as each child's situation is unique.

The information presented in this book emphasizes that teaching infants to sleep through the night is generally advised only for those aged 4 months and older. If you have a newborn or an infant under 4 months of age, it is prudent to postpone any sleep training initiatives. Infants in this age group are typically unable to differentiate between night and day and require regular feedings within a 24-hour cycle for optimal health. Therefore, expecting a newborn to 3-month-old to achieve uninterrupted sleep is not advisable and may lead to unnecessary stress.

Furthermore, do not engage in sleep training for your child if they possess any medical conditions that may hinder their ability to sleep for extended periods.

The American Academy of Pediatrics explicitly advises against bed sharing due to the associated risks, including the potential for harm to the child and the increased risk of Sudden Infant Death Syndrome (SIDS). It is recommended that infants be placed on their backs to sleep in a designated sleep space, such as a crib, bassinet, or portable play yard equipped with a firm, flat mattress and a fitted sheet.

To minimize the risk of suffocation, ensure that loose blankets, pillows, stuffed toys, bumpers, and other soft items are not present in the sleep area. Additionally, avoid placing any items that may obstruct the infant's nose or airway as they move during sleep.

Parents and caregivers should refrain from allowing infants to sleep on couches, armchairs, or in seating devices such as swings or car seats, with the exception of travel in a vehicle. Breastfeeding, if feasible, may help reduce the risk of SIDS, and it is strongly advised to avoid smoking in the vicinity of the infant.

Finally, always review and adhere to the instructions for toys, rockers, or any other devices that support your baby. Register these items and remain vigilant regarding recalls for products utilized with your child to ensure their safety and well-being.

Read Daily to Refuel, Recharge and Energize Yourself

- You will never know everything as a parent and that's OK. Invest in yourself to learn more and grow.

- Moms need enough sleep to heal and thrive.

- Grow your confidence, competence & community to go the distance.

- Lowering your voice is much more effective than yelling at children.

- Take care of yourself so you can take care of others.

- Don't get overwhelmed by the latest parenting trends. Parenting with love and understanding is timeless.

- Sleep is not a luxury but a necessity.

- Use your time with your baby wisely. You only get 936 weeks until they're an adult.

- Activate the leader within you. Do the same for your child.

- Treat your family like it's a team. Encourage each member to shine.

SLEEP FOR YOU AND YOUR BABY

Tip 1: Hire a Baby Sleep Coach

The first few months with a newborn can be exhausting, especially when it comes to sleep. Typically, babies sleep for 2 to 3 hours at a time, wake up to eat, and then go back to sleep. This cycle of eat-sleep-eat-sleep happens around the clock for the first three to three and a half months.

You can hire a baby sleep coach to help you as soon as your baby is born. That's when you can start establishing healthy sleep habits. However, do not expect your baby to sleep all night until they're around 4 months old.

If you don't take steps to help your baby establish good sleep habits early on, you might find yourself struggling to figure it out on your own, which can be stressful and draining. Before joining the Baby Sleep Accelerator™ Coaching Program, many moms were unsure how to get their baby to sleep well at night or during naps before they transformed into moms who could get their baby to sleep 10-12 hours at night.

Some moms try to "wing it" and hope things will improve, but this often leads to more sleepless nights, lack of routine, and even bed-sharing, which can be dangerous. If you want quick and successful results, hiring a baby sleep coach can make all the difference.

BONUS: Go to www.BabySleepAccelerator.com to become a Coaching Insider or **get a gift card to join**!

Tip 2: Create Your 4-Hour Sleep Chunk

More than likely, you'll hear healthcare professionals, loved ones, and well-meaning friends say, "Sleep when your baby sleeps." In theory, it sounds great! But in reality, it's much harder to achieve. Napping every 2-3 hours with your baby can be challenging, especially if you don't have the support to make it happen. Most new moms find themselves needing to tidy up, do laundry for themselves and the baby, prepare meals, run errands, and attend doctor's visits—all while providing round-the-clock care.

If you're barely getting any sleep, consider designating a specific time each night, perhaps between 8:00 PM and 12:00 AM, for someone else to fully care for the baby so you can get a solid four hours of rest. This will require planning for your baby's feeding needs, particularly if you're breastfeeding. In that case, pumping enough milk in advance to cover two feedings during this window is essential. This way, you can wake up at midnight feeling somewhat rested and ready to resume nighttime duties. This four-hour stretch of sleep, though it may seem elusive in those first few months, can make a meaningful difference in how you feel.

Tip 3: Swaddle Blankets Are A Must-Have

Invest in non-weighted swaddle blankets or traditional muslin blankets, as they are excellent for helping your baby sleep better. Swaddling mimics the snugness of the womb, providing comfort and security, which can help soothe a fussy baby.

Non-weighted swaddle blankets allow for breathability and flexibility, reducing the risk of overheating while ensuring your baby feels cozy. Muslin blankets, in particular, are made from lightweight, breathable fabric that stretches easily, making them ideal for swaddling. Their softness helps prevent skin irritation, promoting a more restful sleep for your little one.

It's important to note that the American Academy of Pediatrics advises against using any type of weighted blankets for infants due to safety concerns. By incorporating swaddling into your baby's bedtime routine, you can create a calming environment that encourages longer sleep stretches, ultimately benefiting both your baby's well-being and your own.

Tip 4: Essential Items for Your Baby to Sleep Better

Here are the essentials to help your baby sleep better—must-haves for your toolkit.

First, invest in a baby monitor with a camera, night vision display, and microphone.

You should also have baby books that promote sleep. Examples of sleep inducing books for babies include but not limited to *20 Yawns*, *Love You Forever*, or *The Sleep Book*.

Next, consider **using more brown noise than white noise.** Recent research by Dr. April Benasich, director of the Infancy Studies Laboratory at Rutgers University, has cautioned that white noise may negatively impact children's language.She suggests brown noise could be more beneficial for your baby's brain development than white noise.

White noise is often just a static sound, like a hair dryer or TV static, brown noise has more depth and can resemble soothing sounds like falling rain or ocean waves, which can help your baby sleep better.

Finally, make sure you have comfortable onesies or footed pajamas and a bassinet for your newborn.

Tip 5: Choose a Bath-time for Your Newborn

From the very first day you bring your baby home, you should establish a consistent bathtime in the evening. Use this routine as a tool to help set up healthy sleep habits for your newborn, which will encourage better sleep later on. Aim for a time between 6:00 PM and 7:00 PM so your baby can begin to associate this period with bedtime.

If you want to learn more about creating better sleep habits for your newborn, you can schedule a baby sleep strategy session by heading to www.BabySleepAccelerator.com

Tip 6: Shared Responsibility: Learning Baby Care Together

It's important to teach your spouse or partner how to care for your baby if they don't know how. If they say, "I don't know how to swaddle the baby" or "I can't change a diaper," use this opportunity to encourage learning together. This will help both of you gain the skills needed for caring for your baby.

Allowing your spouse or partner to avoid learning sets a precedent for them to rely on you for answers. The more you learn on your own, the more exhausted you'll feel when you have to go back and teach them later. By learning together, you can reduce frustration and balance the workload.

If you find yourself doing most of the tasks while your spouse or partner says, "You do it better than I can," it can lead to resentment. They may still enjoy their pre-baby life while you handle most responsibilities.

The key is to learn together and not let your spouse or partner take the easy way out by saying, "I just don't know."

how to do it; you do it."

BONUS: Join Baby Sleep Accelerator™ Coaching Program **with your spouse or partner or other caregiver**

SELF-CARE

Tip 7: Hire a Doula

If you are pregnant and you have enough time before your due date to hire a doula... then do it.

A doula is there to provide you with physical and emotional support during your labor. A doula can be a game changer during your labor and delivery, whether you're having a vaginal delivery or a C-section. Having an advocate in the room who is focused on your needs and can help you with natural pain management can make a significant difference. They can demonstrate exercises or positions to help facilitate a smoother delivery and support you in tailoring your birthing experience to your liking.

Some hospitals and birthing centers are more accommodating than others in honoring your birth plans. In such cases, having a doula can help provide invaluable support.

While a doula has limitations because they're not formally trained in obstetrics, they can help you better communicate your plans to those who are, so that your wishes are more likely to be carried out. This support can greatly enhance your overall experience during labor and delivery.

NOTE: While doulas offer invaluable emotional and physical support, **a medical professional's advice will always take precedence over that of a doula, especially regarding medical decisions.** Doulas are there to advocate for you and assist with comfort measures, but their role is not to provide medical care or make decisions related to the health of you or your baby. Always defer to your doctor or healthcare provider for any medical guidance during childbirth.

Tip 8: Schedule Date Nights with Your Significant Other

If you have a spouse or partner, allow yourselves grace during the first month after having your baby. This time is for bonding and adjusting to your new routine. Once your baby reaches about 4 months-old, start incorporating date nights into your calendar.

Taking care of a baby can be draining for both of you, and it's easy to feel like you're just going through the motions. To keep your relationship thriving, aim to schedule a date night every two weeks.

Date night doesn't always have to mean leaving the house. It could be as simple as a candlelit picnic in your living room while your baby sleeps or enjoying a movie night in your basement. Alternatively, you might hire a babysitter to go out to a concert or take a stroll in the park together.

Have at least three reliable babysitters as backups. Identify one as your primary sitter and keep the others as alternatives. This way, you can confidently make plans for date nights.

BONUS: Schedule a date night every two weeks on your digital calendar and share the entry with your significant other.

Tip 9: Resume Having Sex After An All Clear From Healthcare Professional

After giving birth, sex might be the last thing on your mind. At your six-week postpartum checkup, your OB/GYN will typically let you know if you're ready to resume sexual activity, or if you should wait a bit longer. Getting back into the groove after childbirth can feel a little intimidating, but that's completely normal.

As you ease back into intimacy, it's important to also think about family planning and birth control. You can actually get pregnant just weeks after giving birth, even if you're breastfeeding or haven't had your period yet. So, take the time to discuss your options with your doctor, and figure out what method of birth control works best for you.

And when it comes to sex, just take it slow—being gentle and patient with yourself and your partner is key. It's a gradual process, and there's no rush. Plus, remember that sex can have real benefits for you, both physically and emotionally. Sex helps you release endorphins which relaxes you and eases pain.

Tip 10: Create Your Community

Join a mom group or new parent group. You can find many of these online and you can participate in virtual meetups. There are also in-person mommy or daddy meetups. The key is to build your community.

When you're a parent, you may notice that your social circle shifts a bit, especially if your current friends don't have children. It's natural to start connecting with other parents who can relate to your experiences. While your friends without kids may feel a little left out at times, it's important to balance both worlds—maintain your old friendships while also making new connections with parents. That way, you can gain support, share ideas, and grow as a parent while keeping all your relationships in check.

Remember as the saying goes, it takes a village to raise a child!

Tip 11: Choose Your "Postpartum Observer"

It's important to designate someone close to you who you trust as your "postpartum observer." This person can regularly check in on you, especially regarding your mood and overall well-being. If you're experiencing severe mood swings, feeling hopeless, pessimistic, or struggling to sleep (beyond the typical challenges of new parenthood), it's crucial to have someone who can notice these signs and offer support by helping you become more aware of the behavior.

For example, if you're finding it hard to bond with your baby—something that may start slowly for some—this could be a sign of postpartum depression. While everyone's maternal instincts develop differently, difficulty bonding, withdrawing from friends and family, or feeling disconnected could be red flags. More serious symptoms include thoughts of harming yourself or your baby, suicidal thoughts, or persistent physical issues like body aches, cramps, or digestive problems. These symptoms can significantly interfere with your daily life as you navigate the first few months with your newborn.

If weeks or months have passed and you're still struggling to find a rhythm in taking care of yourself and your baby, it's time to reach out to your pediatrician or OB/GYN. Some doctors may have better resources than others, but don't hesitate to ask for help. If you have access to a postpartum coach, they can also offer guidance and support.

Tip 12: Have Your Designated Check-In Buddy On Standby

Designate a friend, family member, or loved one to regularly check in on you once your baby arrives. Ask them to set reminders in their phone for weekly check-ins during the first month and then monthly for the next few months. They can ask how you're feeling emotionally, if you need help around the house, a meal, or just to be there to crack a few jokes so you can share a laugh.

This support can be split among several people to share the responsibility. Having a built-in community of people checking in on you, not just the baby, can make a world of difference. People will often focus on the baby, but it's important that someone also focuses on you.

Tip 13: Reduce Your Mom Guilt

As an expectant or new mom, it's helpful to create a vision for your parenting journey. Whether you want to be a hands-on mom, homeschool, travel, or simply find more balance, having goals in place can guide your decisions.

However, "mom guilt" can sneak in when reality doesn't match your expectations. Mom guilt is that nagging feeling that whatever you're doing isn't enough. It stems from comparing yourself to other moms—whether in real life or on social media—and the pressure to meet impossible expectations. The myth of the "super mom" makes it worse. Ads, social media, and even family members can make you feel like you should always be doing more.

Parent in a way that works for you. You will never know everything as a parent and that's OK. Focus on the basics—keeping your baby healthy and cared for. Let go of guilt around things like letting your baby eat store-bought baby food or putting them in daycare. Whether you're working or staying home, prioritize what's best for you and your family. It's okay to ask for help, take a break, and find your own rhythm.

Tip 14: Your Push Present Acknowledgement and Reminder

If you want a push gift after giving birth, make sure to let your significant other know, especially if you think they might not be inclined to get one.

Give them a gentle reminder that you'd like a gift, or you can go ahead and treat yourself. If money is an issue then suggest less expensive treats that you could enjoy.

There are many gift options out there. Baby sleep coaching is one of the best gifts you can give yourself and your family.

To avoid disappointment, speak up early and provide your partner with a list of gift options to choose from. This way, there's no confusion, and you won't feel let down.

BONUS: Head to https://www.babysleepaccelerator.com/egift-card

Tip 15: Go Low Maintenance For A While

You have a great excuse to keep things low-key regarding your appearance when your baby arrives. Makeup-free pajama days are perfectly acceptable! Limit the use of harsh-smelling products like lotions, perfumes, and hairsprays; opting for more natural scents can soothe both you and your newborn.

Natural scents such as lavender, chamomile, and vanilla are especially calming. For Black women, choosing protective hairstyles like braids can significantly reduce the time spent on your hair, allowing you to focus more on caring for your baby.

When it comes to your nails, it's perfectly fine to keep them natural and trimmed short during the first few weeks after bringing your baby home. You may not have the opportunity to visit a nail salon, so it's essential to keep your nails clean and healthy to avoid accidentally scratching your newborn, especially if you have a broken acrylic nail for instance.

Tip 16: Hire A Lactation Expert

Breastfeeding can be a beautiful and rewarding experience, but it often comes with a unique set of challenges for new moms. In the first few weeks, both you and your baby are navigating a learning curve that can be overwhelming. From figuring out latching challenges that many new mothers encounter to milk supply concerns.

Given these challenges, it's important for new moms to seek support and guidance from lactation consultants or breastfeeding support groups. Having someone to help navigate these early days can make a significant difference in building confidence and ensuring a successful breastfeeding journey.

Tip 17: Get a Kneeling Cushion for Bath Time

Consider getting a kneeling cushion for the bathtub when you're bathing your baby. Sometimes, your baby registry includes everything for the baby but nothing for you. A kneeling cushion is essential for you, your partner, or any caregiver who will be bathing your baby, as it protects your knees during those first few months of bath time.

BONUS: In addition to a bath kneeler, consider getting an elbow cushion as well. These items help prevent discomfort while bathing your baby on hard bathroom floors. If you don't have a sink or a special bath for your baby, it can be even more challenging, making a kneeling cushion all the more important!

Tip 18: Invest in Nursing Clothes

When it comes to breastfeeding, it's important to determine how you want to approach it. Will you need cover-ups while nursing, and are you comfortable breastfeeding in public? If you choose to nurse in public, there are various ways to cover up if you wish. Alternatively, if you feel confident breastfeeding without covering up, that's perfectly fine too!

If you prefer to use cover-ups, there are plenty of nursing-friendly clothing options available, from dresses to shirts, that can help you while breastfeeding. Ultimately, it's about what makes you comfortable. Consider investing in lactation bras and nursing attire to simplify the process.

The last thing you want is to forget about your breastfeeding needs and wear a dress that doesn't allow for easy nursing access at an event! Without the right attire, you may find yourself searching for a secluded spot or restroom to breastfeed. Having nursing dresses or shirts will make it much easier for you to access your baby. Additionally, don't forget to include cover-up blankets and shawls for added privacy.

Tip 19: Add a Bidet for Postpartum Care... You're Welcome!

Bidet: pronounced buh-day (it's French)

Having a bidet for personal hygiene and self-care, particularly during postpartum recovery definitely cleans you up very well and improves your healing especially if you received stitches from tearing. A bidet is a step up from the perineal squirt bottle typically provided if you give birth at a hospital or birth center.

This device, often attached to a toilet, sprays water on your tush and perineal areas after using the restroom. Many bidets allow you to choose between warm or cold water, and more advanced models even blow hot air to dry your intimate regions.

If you developed hemorrhoids during pregnancy or after giving birth, using a bidet can provide significant relief. Again, for all the thank you for this tip... you're welcome!

Benefits:

- **Improved Hygiene:** Offers a more thorough clean than toilet paper, reducing infection risk.

- **Reduced Irritation:** Gentle spray minimizes skin irritation, especially for sensitive areas.

- **Hemorrhoid Relief:** Soothes discomfort and reduces friction for those with hemorrhoids.

- **Encourages Healthy Habits:** Promotes better hygiene practices and infection control.

- **Environmental Benefits:** Decreases toilet paper use, reducing waste and environmental impact.

YOUR MINDSET

Tip 20: Set Boundaries: Embracing Your Inner Leader as a New Parent

When you have a baby, you need to discover the leader inside you. Having a baby means everyone will share their opinions on what you should do and what worked for them. It's important to know how to set boundaries and say "no" when you need to. This helps others respect your choices.

As a mom, it can be tricky when someone you hold in high regard crosses the line. You have all the right to tell others when their advice is overreaching. But it can be a fine line and delicate balancing act. You could say something like, **"I appreciate that you care and I value your perspective. Right now, I'm learning to take things one day at a time. I want you to be part of this journey, so please let me reach out when I'm ready to ask for your advice."**

Get ready for people to give you advice you didn't ask for and unexpected criticism. Many will share what worked for them, but remember, their experiences are not the same as yours. It's normal to face this, so keep setting boundaries and be kind to yourself. Allow yourself time to adjust to being a mom, recover, and take care of yourself.

Tip 21: Remove the Guilt Over Breastfeeding vs. Formula Feeding

Its okay to breastfeed your baby, give them formula, or even do both. Many breastfeeding advocates say "breast is best," but sometimes moms are unable to breastfeed and can only rely on formula. The most important thing is keeping your baby healthy, well-fed, and sleeping well.

If you can't breastfeed, that's perfectly fine. It's normal to feel upset about it, but you shouldn't be hard on yourself for doing what you must to feed your baby. You have every right to change your mind and make different choices as you go along. Your main goal is to help your baby and keep them safe.

Remember, despite what you see online or hear from family and friends, the best choice is whatever works for you and your baby. What matters most is that your baby is alive and well.

Tip 22: Gratitude Note + Gift

Write a "gratitude note" to your parents, a mother or father figure thanking them for the positive impact they had on your life. You can add a gift with the note as well. This act alone is very valuable in expressing thanks for the influence and support you received from them during your upbringing.

As a new parent, you may find yourself butting heads with your parents or in-laws if they may have different opinions on how to care for your baby. These differences in approach could be anything from how to feed your baby to how you should bathe them. Often, your elders' way of doing things may not fit the new way you want to raise your child.

This "gratitude note" can help reconcile potential conflicts based on parenting decisions with your elders. The gift or note may serve as a reminder of your appreciation for everything they've done for you and will continue to do.

Writing this letter can also help you gain perspective. Parenting often evokes memories of your childhood. This process may give you a deeper perspective and appreciation for those who contributed and made sacrifices to take care of you when you were a baby. Saying thank you could go a long way.

If the person you want to thank is deceased you can write a thank you note in your journal as a keepsake.

Gift Ideas for grandparents

- Hats, t-shirts that say grandma/grandpa
- Personalized Christmas ornaments
- Grandparent memory book

Sample Gratitude Note

Dear Mom,

Thank you for everything you've done for me. As I prepare to become a mother, I want to let you know that I truly appreciate all the sacrifices you made to raise me. Your love and guidance have shaped me into who I am today.

I'm so excited for you to be a grandparent! I know you'll share the same warmth and wisdom with my child that you gave to me.

I look forward to sharing this beautiful chapter together as our family expands!

Love,

[Insert Your Name]

Dear Dad,

Thank you for everything you've done for me over the years. Your hard work and dedication have shaped who I am, and I truly appreciate the sacrifices you made to help get me to where I am today.

As I get ready to become a father myself, I can't help but think about the values you instilled in me. I'm excited for you as you become a grandfather.

You were an amazing dad. I look forward to this next chapter in our lives together.

Love,

[Insert Your Name]

Tip 23: Have Your Social Media Plan Ready to Go

Have a plan for your social media consumption and use, especially after you have your baby. Consider how much you want to share about your child and whether you want to be active on social media at all. In the early days, social media can lead you into a trap of comparison. If you find yourself looking at friends who are also having babies and seem to have it all together, remember that social media often presents a curated version of reality.

When you see maternity shoots or adorable newborn pictures of babies bundled up in fuzzy blankets, you don't see the chaos behind the scenes—the crying, the exhaustion, or the photographer dangling toys to coax a smile. All you see is that perfect baby or the seemingly flawless family, which can lead to feelings of inadequacy, especially if you're struggling.

To avoid this downward spiral, establish a plan for your social media use. For example, you might decide to log in just to watch cat videos for a good laugh or to find inspirational quotes that uplift you.

INCREASE YOUR EFFICIENCY

Tip 24: Add Key Dates/Milestones to Electronic Calendars

Start using shared electronic calendars with your spouse, partner, or friends to help keep everyone organized. This is especially useful for planning outings or date nights. Sharing the calendar can help combat "Mom Brain" and reduce forgetfulness. At the end of each day, review the calendar together to discuss upcoming events and changes for the week, month, or year.

Add important dates like birthdays, which will send you email reminders and phone alerts, saving you time and stress. For a visual aid, consider getting a wall calendar to jot down significant dates and help plan your year.

Also, remember to include your baby's projected milestones. For example, set reminders for when your baby turns 3 months old to transition to a stage 2 bottle nipple or upgrade their pajama size. Tracking these milestones ensures you're prepared for your baby's growth and changes, making the transition smoother for both of you.

Examples of electronic calendars:

- Google Calendar
- Outlook Calendar
- Apple Calendar
- Cozi Calendar

BONUS: Consider getting a large wall calendar that shows the entire year at a glance. This can help you see the big picture and remind you that there is light at the end of the tunnel.

Tip 25: Get the Ultimate Cooking Duo: Multi-Cooker & Air Fryer

If you haven't picked up a multi-cooker or an air fryer yet, you really should. They're basically the superheroes in your kitchen, especially when you need to cook healthy meals fast. An air fryer is awesome for making food crispy without using too much oil. An Instant Pot, one of the most popular multi-cookers, for example, can do a bit of everything—pressure cooking, slow cooking, steaming—you name it. These gadgets make life so much easier when you're juggling family meals.

BONUS: Good Housekeeping lists several top-rated multi-cookers including Instant Pot and Ninja air fryers.

Tip 26: Hire A Dog Walker

If you have dogs, consider setting up dog-walking services or asking a friendly neighbor to walk your dogs at least once a day. This can help alleviate the stress of caring for both your baby and your pets.

This way, your dogs can get regular exercise and attention. You get to free up some time to focus on your newborn while maintaining a routine for your furry loved ones.

Tip 27: Set-up Your Meal Delivery Service

Before having a baby, deciding what to eat for yourself or your family is something you do every day. However, once you add the responsibility of caring for a newborn, it becomes much more challenging than you might expect.

Consider setting up meal delivery services or asking friends to provide meals after your baby arrives. If possible, arrange this before your due date or designate a friend to help coordinate meal deliveries.

Encourage your friends and loved ones to let you know when they'll deliver meals or share your preferences with them. Websites like MealTrain.com allow you to organize meal support quickly, enabling friends to sign up to bring you delicious dishes.

You can use delivery services such as DoorDash, Uber Eats, or GrubHub. You might even request DoorDash gift cards from friends if they ask what you'd like for your baby shower.

Tip 28: Prepare Your Frozen Meals Before You Deliver

If you just love cooking your own meals then being proactive can make a significant difference, so consider preparing meals in advance that can be frozen, such as lasagna and other hearty dishes.

Preparing frozen meals before your newborn arrives is crucial, as it ensures you have nutritious options readily available during those hectic early weeks. Having these meals on hand can save you time, money and reduce stress, allowing you to focus on caring for your baby while still providing nourishing food for yourself and your family.

Tip 29: Arrange to Have Your Home Cleaned

If you have the means then go ahead and hire a cleaning service. You can arrange for cleaners to come to your home bi-weekly or monthly, alleviating the pressure of keeping your house clean while you care for your newborn or infant.

It's a good idea to find a cleaner before you give birth, so you won't have to worry about it once your baby arrives. Test them out while you're in the nesting phase when you may get an intense urge to clean everything right before giving birth.

You can also add cleaning services to your baby registry, allowing friends and family to pitch in for this helpful support. Don't feel guilty about using your resources to ease your transition into caring for a newborn. It's perfectly fine to seek assistance during this period.

Keeping your home clean and organized not only reduces stress but also helps you breathe easier and enjoy a better experience while caring for your baby in those first few months.

Tip 30: Consider Adding a Wagon Stroller to Your Baby Registry

In addition to the basics for a new baby or infant, like a stroller, crib, and bassinet, consider investing in a wagon stroller for when your baby gets older, especially if you have older siblings. Wagons are perfect for trips to the park, the beach, or while traveling.

They can be easier to maneuver through an airport than a stroller when you have older children. While you definitely need a stroller for a newborn or infant, wagons are incredibly versatile.

Wagons can help transport groceries from your car to the house or give you a free hand when needed. With a stroller, you typically need both hands to push, but using a baby carrier with a wagon for older kids can make outings much easier.

Wagons are especially handy during the toddler years, so be sure to add one to your baby registry!

BABY CARE

Tip 31: Find the Right Pediatrician for You

Start looking for a pediatrician before your baby arrives. Schedule an appointment to interview potential pediatricians and visit their practices. It's important to choose a pediatrician with whom you have a good rapport with.

It's essential to consider the size of the practice; ask about the average number of patients they see each day. If you choose a fast-paced practice, you might find it challenging to get timely appointments, especially if your baby falls ill and you have to wait a whole day before your sick baby is evaluated.

Look for a practice that offers same-day or virtual appointments, as these options can be more convenient for families with newborns and infants. Some pediatricians utilize a Direct Primary Care model, which involves monthly membership fees and may include exclusive services such as house calls. For higher-income families, some pediatricians operate as a Concierge Practice, charging an annual fee for more personalized services and amenities.

Tip 32: Say Hello to Galactagogue Foods!

Galacta-what? Say it slowly: gal-act-a-gogue (it rhymes with "catalog"). These are substances found in foods that help increase breast milk production.

Some of the top galactagogue foods for moms looking to boost their milk supply include oatmeal, green leafy vegetables like kale, spinach, and arugula, as well as fenugreek, lentils, cashews, and almonds. Personally, I found sweet potatoes to be a clear winner! Try incorporating some of these foods into your diet and see which ones help enhance your lactation.

Tip 33: Have Several Babysitters On-Call

As a new mom, it's important to start looking for babysitters as early as possible. Look for babysitters who are trustworthy and have experience with newborns—whether that's a family member or a professional caregiver. Having someone you can rely on will allow you to take breaks, run errands, or even enjoy a much-needed nap. Being proactive in your search will help ensure that you have reliable support when you need it.

Tip 34: Get Gifts for Older Siblings

Your baby will likely receive many gifts, but don't forget about their older siblings. Add a few gifts to your baby shower registry for them to help them feel included and a part of this special moment.

Get a book or toy for your baby's older sibling. Acknowledge their new role as a big brother or big sister, whether it's their first or fourth time.

Look for books aimed at older siblings about expecting a baby, such as "I'm a Big Sister" or "I'm a Big Brother." These stories can help your older child understand what to expect when bringing home a new sibling and make them feel special by knowing they also receive gifts and attention. This reinforces their importance as part of the family during this exciting transition.

Tip 35: Install Your Baby's Air Purifier

There are many gadgets and tools available to help care for your baby, and one essential item is an air purifier. An air purifier creates a cleaner environment, reducing the risk of respiratory issues and allergies while providing peace of mind regarding your baby's health. Additionally, air purifiers can improve your baby's sleep by ensuring they breathe fresher air, which can lead to more restful nights.

These devices also help minimize the spread of airborne illnesses, such as the flu and colds, by filtering out viruses and bacteria. Importantly, air purifiers can reduce the risk of Sudden Infant Death Syndrome (SIDS). To maximize their effectiveness, place an air purifier in your baby's nursery or in your bedroom if your baby is co-sleeping in a bassinet or crib. Consider having another air purifier in frequently used spaces, like the living room, where your baby spends a lot of time during the day.

BONUS: Carefully read the instructions on how to clean your air purifier to keep it functioning at optimal levels.

Tip 36: Sudocrem for Your Baby's Diaper Rashes

There's an amazing ointment called Sudocrem which is an antiseptic healing cream effective for diaper rash. Sudocrem was developed by a pharmacist in Ireland and has been effective for decades. In Belgium, it is sold under the name Dermocrem.

You can usually find it online from major retailers like Walmart and Amazon. This stuff is incredible! If your baby starts developing a diaper rash, after 24 hours after applying you will see significant improvement.

I've used it for severe diaper rashes on all three of my babies, and it worked like a charm. While it can be pricier than other diaper rash creams, it is great to have during emergencies.

Tip 37: Less Mess For You with a Bum Spatula

If you use diaper creams like Sudocrem that are white, pasty, and downright messy, then having a bum spatula will save you a lot of white smears all over your clothes, your baby's clothes, and your baby's skin.

This tool allows you to apply creams, such as those for preventing diaper rash or petroleum jelly as a skin protectant, without getting your fingers messy. While petroleum jelly is clear and can be easier to wipe off, sometimes you just don't want all that mess on your hands.

Using a bum spatula will save you time and stress, making your life a whole lot easier. Be sure to add one to your baby registry.

BONUS TIP: Pray & Say Your Affirmations

There will be times when you won't know what to do as a parent. Whenever you feel stuck, lost, confused, anxious, sad, or even happy, remember that you can always turn to God in conversation or prayer. Ask for help, guidance, solutions, or wisdom.

Speak affirmations over yourself and your baby daily.

Examples:
- Say: "I am [insert your name], and *good things happen to me all the time.*"
- Say: "I learn new things easily and effortlessly because I am powerful beyond measure."

Acknowledgements

I am grateful to Marilyn Suey CFP, for inspiring me to write this book. Your guidance and encouragement have been invaluable.

I would also like to give special thanks to the following individuals: Nikeba Dawkins, Sophia Denard, Shaneca Williams, Mary Ogunojemite, Tia Miller, Sonnia Ragozin, Sherrian Garcia, Ashleigh Distin, Marley Distin, Alice Fray, MD, Jessica Woghiren, ESQ, Nicole Celso, Annalie Celso, and Lara Wiggins. Your support and insights have enriched this work, and I am deeply grateful for your contributions. Thank you for being a part of this adventure.

Notes

Peanut. (2023). *Invisible Mothers: The State of Invisibility.* Peanut App. https://invisible-mothers.peanut-app.io/

Snuz. (2023) *The Truth About Sleep: Snuz Sleep Survey Results* https://www.snuz.co.uk/blogs/sleep-talk/the-truth-about-sleep-snuz-sleep-survey-results

American Academy of Pediatrics. (2024). *AAP leaders call decision to pull harmful weighted sleep products 'critical step.'* AAP News. https://publications.aap.org/aapnews/news/28768/AAP-leaders-call-decision-to-pull-harmful-weighted?autologincheck=redirected

Lardieri, A. (2024). Exclusive: Trendy parenting technique used by millions could stunt babies' development and cause 'public health issue,' experts warn." The Daily Mail. https://www.dailymail.co.uk/health/article-13781665/trendy-parenting-technique-stunt-baby-development-expert-warning-white-noise.html

Salamon, Maureen. (2023). *What Does a Birth Doula Do?* Harvard Health Publishing: Harvard Medical School. https://www.health.harvard.edu/blog/what-does-a-birth-doula-do-202311222995

Centers for Disease Control and Prevention (CDC). (2024) *Symptoms of Depression Among Women.* CDC's Division of Reproductive Health. https://www.cdc.gov/reproductive-health/depression/index.html

Bemis. (2021). *Bidets for Postpartum: The Benefits of a Bidet After Giving Birth.* BioBidet by Bemis. https://biobidet.com/blogs/news/bidet-for-postpartum

Skylight Frame. (2024). *The 4 Most Popular Digital Family Calendars.* Skylight. https://www.skylightframe.com/blog-popular-digital-family-calendars/?srsltid=AfmBOoo2wB-I57qVoFGM9Xw5LZ9-D9JCkZlgce_EcPGeSO2iRuHOfyMW

Papantoniou, N. (2024) *8 Best Air Fryers, According to Our Testing.* Good Housekeeping. https://www.goodhousekeeping.com/appliances/a24630295/best-air-fryers-reviews

Mendelsohn, H., & Geall, M. (2024). *13 Best Multi-Cookers, Expert Tested.* Good Housekeeping. https://www.goodhousekeeping.com/uk/product-reviews/house-garden/g41583072/best-multi-cookers/

Meal Train. (2024). *Meal Train 101: Everything you need to know about organizing support.* https://www.mealtrain.com/articles/333-meal-train-101-everything-you-need-to-know-about-organizing-support#:~:text=Meal%20Train%20is%20an%20organized,free%20Meal%20Train%20page%20now!

American Academy of Family Physicians (AAFP).(2024). *Direct Primary Care.* AAFP Policy: Direct Primary Care. https://www.aafp.org/family-physician/practice-and-career/delivery-payment-models/direct-primary-care.html

La Leche League. (2023). *Galactagogues.* La Leche League Canada. https://www.lllc.ca/galactagogues

Home Depot. (2024). *How to Clean an Air Purifier.* Home Depot. https://www.homedepot.com/c/ab/how-to-clean-an-air-purifier/9ba683603be9fa5395fab901a8bbbd9d

Brennan, D. (2023). *Are Air Purifiers Safe for Babies?* Grow by WebMD: Health & Pregnancy Guide. https://www.webmd.com/baby/are-air-purifiers-safe-for-babies

Sudocrem. (2024). *Frequently Asked Questions.* Sudocrem. https://sudocrem.ie/faq/antiseptic-healing-cream/

About Nesta

Nesta Lumpkin is America's #1 Baby Sleep Accelerator Coach, a top-selling author, and an engaging speaker. She founded Just Bloom Life, LLC to empower families.

At just 1 year old, Nesta was placed in foster care because her mother didn't have enough support during the postpartum period. This experience fuels Nesta's mission to help moms get their babies to sleep through the night, so they can better manage the demands of caring for their baby, maintaining their career, and nurturing important relationships.

With over a decade of experience in broadcast news writing and production at leading networks such as CNN, CNN International, and HLN, Nesta brings a wealth of knowledge to her work.

She received the prestigious Peabody Award for her production on CNN's coverage of the 2013 Egypt Uprising and has contributed to Emmy Award-winning programming for CNN International. Nesta graduated magna cum laude with a Bachelor of Arts in Journalism: Public Relations from Georgia State University.

Her speaking engagements and writings encourage individuals to explore fresh perspectives on family, with clients praising her work as "powerful and eye-opening."

After 17 years in the industry and experiencing burnout as a writer, Nesta parted ways with CNN. This pivotal moment inspired her to create the Baby Sleep Accelerator™ Coaching Program, designed to help moms avoid burnout and get their babies to sleep through the night, allowing them to function better.

Ready to give a thoughtful gift?

HEAD TO

Babysleepaccelerator.com/egift-card

Baby Sleep Accelerator÷ eGift Card – The Ultimate Gift for Expecting Moms

Searching for the ultimate baby shower gift, push present, Mother's Day surprise, or holiday treat? Give the gift of rest and relief with the Baby Sleep Accelerator™ eGift Card! It's more than just a present—it's the key to helping parents finally get some sleep.

Ready to get 2/7 support during your baby's sleep journey?

HEAD TO

FREEGIFTFROMNESTA.COM

TO BOOK A FREE ($500 VALUE) BABY SLEEP CONSULTATION SESSION

Ready to follow a blueprint to get your baby sleeping 10-12 hours at night?

HEAD TO

BABYSLEEPACCELERATOR.COM

MORE ABOUT THE BABY SLEEP ACCELERATOR÷ COACHING PROGRAM

Live coaching to guide you through NEW easy-to-use methods

Solutions at your fingertips when your baby has sleep disruptions

Meal-plans to aid your baby with more fulfilling sleep

All-day support to help you as your baby starts their customized sleep plan

On Demand Baby Sleep Accelerator™ Coaching Program

Save yourself time, energy and stress by joining

GET NESTA LUMPKIN'S #1
AMAZON BESTSELLING BOOK

Made in the USA
Columbia, SC
07 November 2024